MW01233012

Self Help Easy Mode

Michelle Kolin

INTRODUCTION

"Self Help Easy Mode" is a collection of the best tips and trick that will help you follow your ambitions by setting and achieving your goals in the right way.
You will learn to organize your finances, to focus on your goals, the best ways to achieve them and a lot more.

CONTENTS

Ten Ways To Change Your Life TODAY!

When it comes to changing your life, it can seem like it will take years before you actually make substantial changes. You might feel like giving up before you even get started.

What you need is a way to kick start the changes that you want to make in your life – and here are ten ways to get started today.

#1 Change Your Routine

One of the simplest ways to start improving and changing your life is to change something that you've always done. And it doesn't have to even be related to the goal that you have in mind.

When you want to make changes in your life, you want to get the ball rolling somehow. To get that momentum going, try changing small things in your life today.

For example, have you ever driven to work and not remembered how you've gotten there? Not only is this a scary notion, but it also can be a great lesson in being aware of your surroundings and how they're getting in the way of your self-improvement.

Here are some simple ways to change up your routine today:

- Take a new route to work

- Eat a meal during a different time of day (i.e. eat breakfast at dinnertime)

- Change the order of your exercise routine

- Get up earlier or later than you normally do

- Do different chores around the house or ignore chores that you always do
The point of this exercise is to realize that while we might feel comfortable in our lives, it's that comfort and that 'settling' that might be getting in the way of the changes that we want to make.
Start the changes right now by changing other, not-as-important parts of your life.
You may be surprised at how different the world looks and much more likely you are to believe that bigger changes are indeed possible.

#2 Look in your closet

In Feng Shui decorating principles, when you use certain colors and positions of furniture in your house, you can affect greater changes in your life. Taking this idea a step further, when you want to change something about your life for the better, doesn't it make sense to start changing your surroundings?

A simple way to do this (without spending your money redecorating your house) is to simply change your appearance for a day.

You can do this by simply getting out of your clothing rut and trying something that is completely unlike you. For example, if you wear black all the time, try wearing a bright and boisterous color. If you're someone that likes to wear colorful outfits, try something more toned down.

The point is to approach your outfit as you would your life – by changing it.

Your outward appearance can make your feel more confident in yourself because you know that you look as good as you feel or at least, as you want to feel. And that confidence will show up in your actions as well as your interactions with others.

People can't help but respond to change. When others notice that you are holding your head differently, they will begin to respond in kind. This is why you will hear the term, 'power suit' quite often. By putting on a costume of sorts, you can create a new you – a more powerful you.

If you feel that you don't have anything in your closet to wear that will help you feel differently, it's time to start thinking about new ways of wearing certain pieces of clothing together. Maybe you can simply wear a crazy pair of socks under your classic business suit. Or perhaps you can choose larger earrings or a silly necktie.

Whatever makes you feel differently about yourself, try to incorporate that into the way that you're dressing yourself today.

Here are some other ideas:

- Wear a skirt instead of pants (ladies, of course)

- Try a different shirt with a suit – one that you've never paired together before

- Wear a scarf to accessorize

Wear a different piece of jewelry
Go to the back of your closet to see what you can

find – it just might change your life.

#3 Don't lie

What would your day be like if you didn't lie about anything? Think about it for a moment. We all seem to lie about something during out day, even if we don't realize it. When our food comes at a restaurant, we might say that there's nothing else that we want, even if the wrong order comes out. Or when we're heading to a movie, we might say to our friend or partner that we really don't care what show we're going to, even if there's one that we really want to see.
Why do we do this? Because we don't want to hurt someone's feelings.
However, in most cases of lying, what we're really doing is not being truthful with ourselves and our needs. By considering what someone else thinks, we can place the responsibility for our happiness on someone else's choice – and one that typically doesn't match our own preferences.
On the other hand, when we lie, we're also not taking responsibility for our own actions and their consequences. When we lie to our boss about a project or the bill collector, we're avoiding the issue at hand – and now allowing ourselves to learn from the mistake.
To change your life, you need to stop lying to yourself and everyone around you. This isn't to say that it won't be a tricky thing, but it will be something that will dramatically change the way

that you approach your life.

Not lying for one day will make you slow down and really think about everything you're about to say and why you're saying it. In doing so, this will create an opportunity for you to learn more about the way you think and where you might need to make changes in that thinking.

For example, when you stop lying about whether or not you can talk to someone on the phone, you might find that people that you really don't care to talk to can be asked to call back at another time, leaving you time and energy to do the things that you really want to do.

And that creates the space for you make the changes that you need to make.

Some call it 'authenticity' while others call it being an honest person; in any case, trying to be true to your self and to others is a simple way to instigate a new way of living.

#4 Think like an optimist

Many experts will tell you that when you change the way you look at things, you will change your life – and it's true. If you're sitting around expecting the worst of things, you'll be certain to find the worst of things. You'll find all of your mistakes along the way to your goals. You'll notice all of the problems with your plan. And then you'll stop trying because you've noticed that everything is going wrong.

This is where a lot of people fumble on the way to their happiness and the changes that they want to make. By trying so hard to recognize the bad things in their life, they forget about those things that are working well.

For just one day, try to see your life through the eyes of an optimist – a complete optimist. This might seem silly at first, but what you're doing is bringing another perspective, an objective perspective into your view of the world.

Optimists look at the world as though it only has good things to offer and in that thinking, they see the opportunities for learning and growth, rather than the obstacles in their way. Instead of getting upset about the car that cut them off in traffic, they hope that there wasn't an emergency that caused the driver to need to go so fast.

Optimism takes practice. What you might want to do is start thinking about your life as though it were the life of a good friend that you have. When you sense that something is wrong in your day, try to change your thinking to being more positive. For example, when your friend loses his or her job, you don't tell her that it was because they were the worst employee (though you might tell yourself this), you tell them that it wasn't their fault and that there must have been another reason.

When you start treating yourself and your life the way that you would treat a good friend, you start to see possibility in life, rather than problems.

An optimist is simply someone that strives to look for the good in everything. Just for today, you can try to do the same. Is it a realistic way to be every day? Who knows? But what you are doing is allowing your life to be as wonderful as you want it to be, and maybe as wonderful as it already is. You just weren't looking for it.

#5 Don't have any expectations

How many times have you been disappointed? Probably hundreds of times, right? However, if you think back to your times of pain and loss, many of these instances were the direct result of having some goal in mind that wasn't reached or some expectation that wasn't met.

What if you gave up your expectations for a day? For one day, what if you said that you don't really care about what happens?

When you start to attach how you feel to something that's out of your control, you are setting yourself up for feeling badly. There's nothing wrong with having goals and wanting certain things, but when you start relying on the outcome to derive any happiness from it, you can actually be stifling change and growth in your life.

In truth, expectations are just wishes and hopes. There's nothing wrong with them, but many of these same thoughts are based on a number of factors that you can not control – even if you try to.

For example, you can't control how someone reacts to something that you do or say. People are autonomous and will respond in any way that they see fit. When we start to attach our personal feelings on how someone else reacts, we are setting ourselves up for feeling bad about our lives and our selves.

The point of eliminating expectations is to start focusing on what's happening right now – what you can control and what you can't. If you're in a bad situation at work and your boss is yelling at you, you can't control that. However, you can control how good of a job you do – though your boss might still yell at you anyways.

Just for today, try to remember that all that you have in your life is what is right in front of you. Step back and recognize that true change can only come when you stop making it the end all, be all of your existence. If you're trying to lose weight, for example, all you can do right now is eat better right now. You can't expect that the meal that you eat today will affect you weight loss in the future.

Nor can you expect that the one chocolate bar that you have today will ruin your chances of weight loss.

Try to understand that expectations to which you attach your self-worth and self-esteem are generally not worth meeting. It's not about not setting goals for yourself, it's about not making the bar so terribly high.

#6 Make a mistake

Too often, you can start to believe that making changes in your life means that you have to be perfect. However, logically, you know that no one is perfect, even if they seem to be. Perfection has become a burden that we have placed on ourselves – even though it's not realistic.

We all make mistakes along the way to our dreams, so why not give ourselves permission to get things wrong once in a while?

Just for a day, try to remind yourself that it's okay to make mistakes. In fact, try to make one mistake during the day and see what happens. Does the world come tumbling down? Do people hate you for not being perfect? Probably not.

Giving yourself a break is a great way to start changing your life. You're acknowledging that things aren't always going to head in the exact right direction, but that you will make it there – even if there are some shortcuts along the way.

When you start to relieve yourself of being perfect, you can begin to take chances and take steps toward the changes that you want to make because you're not held back by the fear that you might be wrong. Being wrong is okay. You actually need the lesson of getting something wrong once in a while – that's how you'll learn what's right for you.

Think of how much lighter you will feel once you realize that people really aren't watching your every move, or waiting for you to fail – you're the only one that's doing that to your self. Instead, allow yourself to falter, to tumble, and even to fall once in a while.

The real lesson in this tip to change your life is that you have to also learn how to not berate yourself each time you do make a mistake. Instead, try to look at your issues as learning experiences. When you make a mistake, think about what happened and how you might be able to avoid that problem in the future. It's not about creating perfection, but it is about learning how to do better for your self.

You're going to make mistakes as you begin to change your life or parts of your life, but when you start to recognize that it's not a bad thing, you can start moving past problems more quickly and keep on, keeping on.

#7 Talk to a stranger

Although the world is more connected than ever was before - with the inventions of the Internet and cellular phones - it seems that we've become more disconnected. We seem to forget that we aren't the only ones that walk down out streets or have problems. And this might be hindering your ability to change your life.

The truth of the matter is that we aren't alone, though we want to believe that we are. And once we realize that we do have others around us that understand our dissatisfaction with our lives, we can start to make the necessary changes in our own.

Reaching out to people is problematic, however, because it's just not necessary anymore. We can e-mail people or call them on the phone, but it's the real life connections that will truly remind us of the place of others in our lives.

There are a number of ways to reestablish this connection with the world:

- Talk to the cashier at the coffee shop

- Call a friend

- Meet up with your partner outside of the house

Go for a walk outside

These simple ideas can help create the realization that you're not alone in your want to change the way that you live. In fact, establishing a connection with someone with similar goals can help you more easily achieve your own.

If this isn't possible though, at least be sure to reach out and talk to someone once during your day. Make eye contact with them and genuinely care about them – if only for thirty seconds. The point is to reach out beyond your self in order to find that other perspective.

For example, the cashier at your local grocery store that isn't being friendly might be having a horrible time in their lives. And while you used to interpret this rudeness as a slight to you, perhaps taking the time to ask about their day will be the impetus that they need to change their situation. And in doing so, you can help to recognize where you are in the world, how you can continue to make changes to affect your self as well as others.

#8 Quit your job

You don't actually need to quit your job in order to change your life, but if you're not happy about the job that you have, what are you still doing there? The object of this tip is to help your recognize things that you are settling for instead of making room for the things that you'll really enjoy having in your life.

Maybe it's not that you need to quit your job, but it's that you need to quit your attachment to it. Many of us believe that when we do a good job at work, we're good people who are successful and deserve to be happy. But when our jobs don't satisfy us, we believe that we don't deserve to be happy.

It is in this cycle, or others like it, that we begin to feel like less of a person that can make changes in our life. So, to stop this cycle, we need to recognize that we are not what we do or what we accomplish.

In effect, you will want to quit the power that your job has over you.

But how to do this? To quit the power that your job has over you, you will want to consider the following pieces of advice:

- Try not to judge yourself by what you can accomplish

- Create a to do list, but make priorities

- Set the bar lower

- Recognize that what you need from the job and what your boss needs from the job are completely different

- Try to establish a consistent work schedule

- Leave work at work

- Realize that work is just work
  While that sounds like a lot of platitudes, one of the biggest lessons in the bunch is the idea that work is just work. It can help for you to realize that while something at work might seem like a major concern right now, chances are likely that in six months from now, it won't seem like such a big deal. Just for today, try to think about your job as though it was the last day that you were working. How does that feel?
  You don't have to quit your job to quit the hold that it exerts upon you; but if you find that you can't seem to do this on your own, maybe it is time to at least look at the classified ads for a better place for you.

#9 Find an old hobby

Remember when you were a kid and you wanted to be a basketball player? You went to the garage and started to bounce a basketball up and down. You didn't think about how good you really were at it; you just wanted to do it because it made you happy.

When you want to make bigger changes in your life, you will want to find a way to distract yourself from thinking negative thoughts. And this is why often times, experts will recommend that you pick up a hobby to fill your mind when you're feeling a little less than motivated to change.

There are plenty of things that you can do:

- Knitting

- Sports

- Scrap booking

- Weights

- Crafts

- Etc.
  These can all help you create a different focus for your mind when you're considering change or in the midst of making major changes in your life. Some experts have also noted that when you are trying to break a habit, you will need to fill that time with something else, or else that habit can easily return.
  For example, smokers that are trying to quit often gain weight because they replace their cigarettes with food. But smokers that turn to exercise or other hobbies often do not gain weight as they are replacing the 'bad' habit with a good one.

What you may want to do just for today is replace the thing that you want to change with something else. If you're looking to change your diet to vegetarian, try not eating meat for a day. If you're thinking about going back to school, try reading a book that might be associated with your course of study.

When you start to change the way that you are living your current life, you will start to see new ideas and ways that you can change your life – and it won't seem as scary.

#10 Thank someone that you love

When we're changing ourselves, we forget how often others have stood by us when we weren't in the best of places in our lives. Instead of taking this support system for granted, today is a great time to thank the people that you love.

While it sounds a little corny, just going around to people and thanking them for their support and their understanding can start to solidify the changes that you want to make. You are, in a sense, creating a new life by apologizing for the old life and moving forward.

But when you start to thank others for supporting you, you are also gathering their support for the change that lay ahead. You are readying yourself as well as them for a new and improved you –

one that realizes that mistakes were made in the past, but wants to move forward.

Support is something that we all need, even if we are focused on making changes on our own. The truth is that we aren't always going to be as strong as we need to be. There will be days when we will need someone to help us change our perspective or approach things differently.

When you're trying to change the way that you live or the things that you do, you need all the support that you can get. Starting off by simply thanking people for what they've already done for you is something that doesn't take any time, and makes everyone feel good about the future.

The idea of change is one that we are frightened of. It signifies moving away from what has 'worked' for us in the past and moving towards something unfamiliar. However, when you stop to just make smaller changes in your daily life, you can start the process more easily. Change doesn't have to be startling and unnerving; it can be as simple as doing something different than you would have before: reading a new book or driving a new route to work. However, in these smaller changes, you can find the strength for the bigger changes.

If you can start with the little parts of yourself that you thought didn't matter, just imagine what you can do with the rest of your dreams and goals.

The Use Of Emotional Intelligence in Student Retention

Meeting the higher demands on studying doesn't end with innate mental intelligence. It also requires the various abilities that a person may posses. For one, emotional intelligence largely contributes to a person's ability to cope up with the present trends.

While there may not be a direct link between a student's retention capacity and his emotional intelligence, it is still agreeable that students equipped with the proper level of emotional intelligence are more likely to succeed academically than those who have relatively high IQ yet lack EQ.

Having higher emotional intelligence would provide better coping mechanisms for students. Emotional intelligence is said to be a better determining factor when qualifying the success of a person at any field.

Being emotionally intelligent means that one has the greater capacity to understand himself and the world at which he lives in. It may not be emotional intelligence that would encourage a student to have more focus on the subject matter which in turn would help him retain information. Yet knowing the importance of focus may be learned through having a suitable emotional intelligence.

Emotionally intelligent students are likely to show confidence and self trust. They are also said to have the higher capacity to handle problems more easily and to perform better in terms of academics, given that they are also endowed with an ideal level of intellect. All these, when combined will contribute to a person's self-belief and confidence that will move him to perform better in class.

We should not focus on the student retention alone. There are various factors that must be considered to help determine the extent of value multiple intelligence has in academic pursuits of students. Say for communication among students and working in groups. Those who have higher emotional intelligence are seen to perform better in these parts since they have developed empathy and a number of other social skills.

Emotionally intelligent students are basically those who have natural tendencies to understand other people's emotions and to empathize with them, they are also those who know themselves fully and have the capability to influence other people's emotions and actions. Students equipped with higher emotional intelligence also have the tendency to be a bit more conscious of themselves and others. Thus, they create better relationships with themselves and with those they are closely related to. These among with other issues, when inept may cause obstructions in learning and thus, in retaining students.

Many may view economy as the bane of student retention but what we normally overlook is the incapacities students may present in academic pursuits.

Those who are deficient in emotional intelligence are observed to display behaviors that would link to their exit from higher education, more specifically college. They are those who were not able to tide the increasing pressure of quitting college. There are various stimuli that would eventually lead to the drop out of a student. If we were to sum them up though, we would find that the majority of them are all rooted from lack of emotional intelligence.

Many drop out from college due to failing grades or in the case of ladies, due to pregnancy. If we were to look at these two conditions, it would be easy to conclude that they may actually have stemmed out from deficient EQ.

Therefore, it is not only in personal lives that developing EQ is productive. The cumulative value of which in a four-year institution will be a good determinant of its failure or success.

Life Coach Weekend Certification

If you were a life coach by profession, would you not mind getting certification to prove your point? Several states across the country are already strictly pushing the regulation of getting a certification for this kind of profession. Life coaching career is a particularly dynamic field so you will need to be capable of being flexible. You must ensure that you are capable of actually provide help to the people who need it most and to be able to create drastic positive changes in their lives and in their careers. It's like a domino effect. You help other people gain their personal successes while you also work on your own gains.

The life coach weekend certification is inherently not cheap. For one, you will be cutting down the required eighteen-month period for the accomplishment of the prerequisites. Meaning to say, you will have to invest greater amount of money to get certification faster. Some websites will give you quotes for the life coach weekend certificate that ranges between $4,000 and $8,000.

Most certification awarding firms and agencies henceforth have other fees to be incurred which may be the double of the initial payment made.

Life coaching is a new entry in the corporate world but its fame is rising continuously.

Some of the life coach certification agencies are unable to battle the challenges posed by time itself. They come up and then get abolished in no time because of the lack of credibility to handle the business field. Therefore, you must be very careful when choosing the agency or firm where you will work your life coach weekend certification with.

As a life coach, you must understand the vital relation of the cognitive skills and knowledge to your career. These factors are much important than the existing habits and attitudes you have.

Your skills and knowledge are much more empowered by your educational and training experiences as you gain more mastery through time. This explains the occurrence of failure and incompetence. Logically speaking, a life coach who is well abreast with the ins and outs as well as the ups and downs of life coaching will be able to determine all his strengths and weaknesses. And no one is highly responsible other than yourself for all your personal gains and failures in line with your career.

Having a life coach certification is actually a plus point to you because it only shows that you are competent enough to handle such task. (But it is unfair to set aside the competence of other people who may in truth are uncertified life coaches but in reality, they are actually really good in their fields.)

Life coach trainings will equip you with the necessary tools and processes as well as the effective approaches that will work well with the diversified kinds of clients that may come your way. When properly executed and good strategies are employed, life coaching is expected to create a positive output.

Life coaching can be a rewarding career if only you know how to be in control of the things around you. Know how to play the game and know how to handle your clients. But before you go on with the practice, might as well get a certification as clients put more trust on certified life coaches. They will not opt to waste money for nothing.

The Meaning Of The Fruits Of Pure Happiness

Any dictionary will give you the definition of happiness as an emotional feeling which parallels with joy, contentment, and pleasure. But then these things can thus be temporary. It matters to dig deeper into the real meaning of happiness a happiness that is pure and long lasting.

What makes you happy? Is it the material things such as money, clothes, signature footwear and bags? Do you go for long-term states of happiness such as security, stable health, and love? Which do you value the most? Have you gained access to pure happiness? When was the last time you felt pure happiness? Have you given your all to a certain endeavor and you felt satisfied with all those efforts you've placed?

Pure happiness is said to be both an inner glow and an outer radiation that you can feel together with an utmost satisfaction.

Recognizing pure happiness is a must. There are several occurrences when you have been misled to the real deal with pure happiness and simple pleasure. To mark a definition between the two, it is vital that you know the exact difference that comes with the two terms. Pleasure is a thing of feeling terrific over something. Examples of pleasurable experiences are a vacation over the holidays, a spa treat during the weekend, a good basketball game, and so on. Meanwhile, pure happiness is far from feeling emotionally at ease. It goes more beyond enjoyment. In pure happiness lies contentment and engrossment.

So what is it that let people have pure happiness? Researchers have identified factors that can fully describe pure happiness in a person. They say that people from all walks of life experience true happiness but are just too occupied to pay any attention to it simply because they fail to recognize what pure happiness and pleasure mean.

Among the significant clues of pure happiness are being totally immersed with what you are doing, when you have your full participation on an event or engagement, when you are enjoying to the extreme but you've certainly got no idea with regards to the time, to the passing day, to the other occurrences taking place in your surroundings, and the genuine satisfaction that you feel. These are the instances that can tell you that you've got nothing but pure happiness in your mind and heart.

Pure happiness is actually a state wherein you feel like going along with the flow. You seem to be going along with the rock and roll that sets off smoothly, hassle-free, and effortlessly. It can be compared to an experience wherein the ticking of the clock suddenly stops and you become totally oblivious of the things that go on around you.

Pure happiness is a great feeling of satisfaction which is totally incomparable to the simple pleasures you get when you see your favorite baseball team winning. Pure happiness is felt when you overcome a challenge which has been posed to you.

There is chance of pure happiness for every individual. Do not be taken aback by the negative thought that pure happiness is only meant for other people. You deserve to experience pure happiness. When pure happiness comes your way, you can attest to how blessed you are as a person. Therefore, take time to reconcile things and occurrences in your life. Never fail to give importance to the value of pure happiness.

Train To Be A Life Coach

Many people believe on the expertise and the great help of life coaches. Who are the life coaches? What do they do? Generally, the life coaches are those transformation experts who are oftentimes referred to as magicians because they are that devoted to their clients in terms of guiding them towards the right path to success. Life coaching requires great commitment. So if you think you are ready to face the challenges ahead, then, train to be a life coach!

First, for you to train to become a life coach, you must apply in the CFLC program. But before that, you have to be able to complete the necessary application prerequisites that the course asks for. The requirements must be accomplished in a span of eighteen months with an option to complete the in a shorter time depending on your desire and what you see is most apt for you.

Among the included training is attending the Fearless Foundation Weekend. This will teach you to overcome your fears in order for you to finally realize your hidden potentials. You will also be tasked to participate in the Creating and Leading a Fear Buster Group that will help you out in integrating all philosophies involved in fearless living. During the course, you will be into the most possible situations that will arise at the time of the coaching sessions.

The training to be a life coach, likewise, requires you to be into a minimum of six coaching sessions to obtain the letter of recommendation that will come from the Program Prerequisite Approved CFLC. The people behind the firm possess special training that will all the more enhance your understanding and enrich your knowledge about the real task of a life coach. In turn, they will give you the right edge.

Training to be a life coach also includes insights on how you will be able to get the most potential clients. Do not simply be overwhelmed by the feeling of managing and controlling your own task and helping out people. This kind of task of course is faced with a bunch of difficulties.

It is not as easy as having your business or calling cards made and distributed and you expect that your appointment book will automatically be filled up with names of clients. The schools that offer you the training to be a life coach will not necessarily give you a list of potential clients but they will assist you with regards to how you will be able to harbor clients within your midst. You should bear in mind that you are the sole responsible person who will take charge of your income and success inflow.

Networking and self-promotion are big deals when it comes to attracting clients. A means of clientele will be most possible as you network with friends, acquaintances, by placing ads, participating in forums, building professional relationships and seeping in through networking groups, and a lot of other creative manners that can come into your mind.

Your popularity as a life coach will soon bloom as you earn a good rapport with your clients and through their referrals too. These things will take time. They don't happen overnight. But then, you should be prepared always. Through all these, the training to be a life coach will open your doors to success.

What Is Emotional Intelligence

Being a relatively new area in psychology, emotional intelligence is still on its way to be fully recognized. It is likely that you may find various definitions of emotional intelligence since many experts are still on the disagreement of what this area of intelligence truly measures. However, it is clear that lately, people have shown signs of great interest on this area of personality since they create fruitful products in them.

Intelligence and cognition are two distinctly separated components of human intelligence. IQ is the parameter of measuring cognitive capacities and is said to be constant at any moment it is measured. It may be improved and maximized though. Nonetheless, it would still be limited by the constant value the Intellectual Quotient presents. Say, if a person has an IQ score of 118, then it is possible that this would remain the same throughout the person's life. A change of a point or two may occur perhaps due to developmental factors or margin of error given to a specific IQ test.

But the case is different with Emotional Intelligence

It has been observed how quickly one change from a single emotion to another. But this of course depends on the person subjected to the test or in a given situation. We all react differently to different conditions and there is till no concrete parameter available. Emotions themselves are inconsistent. They largely depend with the person experiencing them.

Due to inconsistencies, no one can still accurately determine how to measure emotional intelligence fully. There is no complete demarcation line between knowledge and intelligence (using the parallelism to describe emotions). Various definitions say the emotional intelligence is dynamic and changes invariably depending on what condition the person is faced to. It therefore, can be increased or decreased, at times it may even be lost. Other experts disagree saying that emotions are stable and therefore, cannot be affected by any condition.

One thing is central to these though, emotions are developed and we are not innately equipped with them at the time of childbirth. Emotions were not even implanted in us during our prenatal stage nor are they recorded in our genes. In a way, they are developed only according to the experiences we had during growth. They only arise when specific stimuli arise.

Emotional intelligence is the capacity of an individual to define his own emotions and to become sensitive to those that he perceives from the environment and the circle of people he is interacting with. It may also be that emotional intelligence is the use of knowledge of these emotions to control situations and create plans and decisions based on the perceived emotions. Other resources would further add that emotional intelligence is part of our personality that dictates us to become more aware of what triggered a specific reaction, both done by the self and people surrounding the "self". It is also known to be the use of emotions to reason out.

There are too many definitions on what emotional intelligence truly is. So far, we have gathered two constants, emotion and understanding the context and concepts of emotions.

In the end, emotional intelligence is much too focused on one's understanding and utilization of his or her emotions and in identification of another person's emotions. These combined will help him determine the proper actions he must make in order to create viable decisions. But emotional intelligence is of course, broader than this interpretation.

Creative Notions

We are all creative beings just as the ultimate being is the divine creator. To create something is to bring into existence something that did not exist before. Creative genius comes when you bring into existence something that will enhance the lives of all who encounter your creation, including yourself. In order to tap your creative genius, there are a few considerations that you should be aware of.

There is one thing that your creative energy demands a lot of and that is time. You have to allow yourself enough space for your creative energies to flow. Some people are fortunate to have a form of employment which requires them to apply their creative minds on a regular basis. If you are a teacher you will continually creating new ways in which to impart knowledge to individual children. The best teachers are always creative geniuses. Others of us are in jobs that only require a certain set of skills. After we have acquired the skills we keep on applying them over and over again without much room for creative thinking. If you fall into this category then you will need to set aside separate time in which to work creatively.

Finding extra time is not always easy with modern daily schedules. Work, travel, family, health, are all things which take precedence over our time.

After these priorities are attended to we are often too spent to begin thinking creatively about anything. The problem is that when we are not able to apply our creativity, which is an inherent drive within all of us, we become dissatisfied and unfulfilled. Sometimes we encounter disgruntled people in the work place and those who appear to hate their jobs. These people are often expressing the deep dissatisfaction they feel at not being able to express themselves more creatively in their lives.

To avoid becoming dissatisfied you must apply yourself creatively. The best way to do this, if you have a very busy schedule, is to channel your creative energy into those things you have to do everyday. A good example of this is food. Cooking is an excellent way to get creative and many of us have to do it everyday. Instead of preparing the same old meals everyday or relying on supermarket ready prepared selections you can create new ways in which you and your family enjoy food and stay healthy. If you travel to work everyday by bus or train you might use this bit of regularly occurring time to read. Reading inspires creativity and you can use the reading time to read something that will teach you something new about what you are interested in.

Although being creative is time consuming it can also be very relaxing. After a hard day at work, instead of slumping in front of the TV for the next 3 hours, you can use this relaxation period to apply yourself creatively. If painting or flower arranging or writing is your thing, this is a very good time to allocate toward pursuing such creative hobbies.

Those who do have a bit of extra time to spend being creative can consider attending a course or group that specializes in their chosen creative pursuit. Other people who are interested in the same thing as you are and who express themselves creatively in a similar way to you, provide a wonderful resource of creative energy which you can draw on to fire up your own creative thinking. Other members will be drawing from you too, everyone contributes and everyone benefits.

It is always a good strategy, for those who are able, to take time to visit somewhere else away from home. If you are able to get away to areas of outstanding natural beauty for example, you should find that the environment inspires you creatively. It is no coincidence that many artists have produced some of their best work in some of the world's most fabulous locations.

The way to tap your creativity is to try to think creatively as much as you can even while occupied with mundane, non-creative activities. You should also understand that creative energy needs to be fed by time; you must find as much time as you can to apply your creative thinking otherwise you might not blossom into the creative genius you are capable of being.

Unlock Your Self Improvement Power

To unlock the infinite power of self you must understand what Self is. Your self consists of three core elements: your body your mind and your spirit. You must work on each one of these elements as part of the self improvement process. Each part of self affects the other and each is as important as the other.

Self Improvement Through Body

Your body is the vehicle with which you interact with physical life. Through your body you communicate with the world around you. Your mind uses your body to express itself, your spirit uses your body to experience itself. You must keep your body as fit and active as it is possible for it to be for the rest of your life. Improve your diet. There is so much information on nutrition and health. Feed your body so that it can perform at an optimal level everyday. Your body includes your hair and skin, your heart, your blood, your respiratory system and your hormones. What are the foods that you need to be consuming that keep these parts of the body functioning at their peak - always?

Your body was built as a strong active working machine. It has been constructed for a potential life of well over a hundred years. If you do not let your body do what it was designed for it will falter and ultimately fail. As well as feeding body for optimum health you must also exercise it so that it can renew itself. Your muscles keep themselves strong by use. The same can be said of your brain too.

Self Improvement Through Mind

It is through the mind that you make the decisions for your body. Everything that you are today has been planned out by your mind. The job you do, how much you earn, the person you married, your weight, your beauty, your car, your house etc, etc. Through your mind and your thoughts you have created your present life experience. If you want self improvement any part of your life as you experience it now you must improve your mind. Knowledge is a key that opens so many doors. Improve your mind through the acquisition of information. Perhaps you want a better job and to earn more money. What do you need to know to get from where you are to where you want to get to? Do you need extra qualifications or to retrain?

However improving the conscious mind is the easier part. The difficulty is the subconscious mind which also has a huge part to play in your life as you experience it today. Perhaps you are overweight because you eat inappropriately. You find it difficult to resist the urge to binge on chocolate but you don't know why. The answer probably lies somewhere in your subconscious where you have stored learned behavior from the past. Once you access the subconscious you can change what is stored there and thus improve your behavior. There are a number of professionals and therapies who can help you improve your self through the mind and there are a number of self help techniques you can use.

Self Improvement Through Spirit

Such concepts as faith, hope, joy, contentment, peace, and love all fall within the realm of the spirit. You don't have to be religious to know the essential nature of these things to fully experience a life of the highest quality. However working with the spirit is different than working with the body and mind. You can work to improve you body and mind but you must work to let your spirit improve you. Just taking time on a regular basis to get in touch with your spirit will bring you self improvement at the most profound level. Religious structures and practices have been put in place by our ancestors to help us commune with the spirit. You may choose to follow a religion or find your own path but without good spiritual health you will find the power of self improvement in all areas much more difficult to unleash.

Achieving Self Improvement

The kind of competitive environment we live in today calls for a little something extra from all of us. Simply having a college degree does not seem to be as important as before, anymore, as most workplaces look for hirees and candidates that have an additional skill or interest before they take them under their wings.

Whether it's a proficiency in particular software or a fluency in more than one language, employers are now obviously more impressed with someone with longer credentials.

Self improvement, however, does not just mean being equipping one's self with additional office-related skills. It can also entail learning another hobby, like knitting, candle-making, or carpentry, or participating in a new group, like Greenpeace, a dance troupe, or a drama class. Whatever it is, it's goal is to help you achieve or learn something greater than what you already know and have.

Everyone would want to improve themselves. There isn't anybody in this world who would refuse an opportunity to be better at something, given man's nature of being always dissatisfied with his or her personal circumstances. Someone somewhere in the world would definitely like to have a better life, dream of getting a new car, fantasize about learning how to swim or do water ballet and imagine being able to multiply three digit numbers in less than 10 seconds.

In addition, self improvement is also a quest to get recognized and appreciated more. People are often dissatisfied with themselves and what they have because they feel envious of other people's fortune. They seek to improve themselves because they want to be at the spotlight even for just a short time, or, if they don't like that much attention, at least have somebody pat them on the back and tell them they have done a good job.

It is a way to reassure oneself that his or her capacity to learn is not limited and that he or she has the ability to advance and grow if only he or she puts his or her mind and heart into the undertaking.

Self improvement is not about beating everyone else in the game of life. It means being happy and satisfied with one's self. It means that life actually has a lot more to offer all of us than what we are currently enjoying and that we have the ability to achieve this if we work at it.

Self Improvement Plan

Making a self-improvement plan and living based on it are probably some of the best things that a person can do for himself. No one else will benefit but him. In most cases, the self is taken for granted and as soon as the person realizes it, it is too late already. Thus, it is ideal that you start the soonest possible time with your self-improvement plan and bring out the best in you and in your life.

However, one does not easily get the realization and encouragement to improve one's self. It really takes a lot of humility and desire for personal growth. What happens normally is that a person, at the very start, is afraid to make a decision on self-improvement. There are a lot of factors causing this kind of hindrance.

A person has the tendency to think that self-improvement is not purely his responsibility. He points out to other people, blaming them for the misfortunes and unpleasant circumstances in his life. Thus, any self-improvement plan will become successful only if a person admits to himself that everything relies on him and he is the only one who has the power to make himself better. All self-improvement plans start from within.

As soon as the desire to improve is there, the rest of the process will be easy. This is especially the case if things are planned properly. A good self-improvement plan must spring out from a personal knowledge of what one specifically wants to improve. There are several possible categories for this. It can be an improvement on one's career, finances, health and fitness, relationships, and many others. Breaking it down to these categories will further align and focus the plan.

The creation of a categorized plan should serve as a guide but should still leave some room for flexibility. This is important to note as there is no such thing as a definite line of events. Circumstances do change and unpredictability of happenings in one's life is inevitable. A great level of patience and perseverance what must be involved no matter what in any effort towards self-improvement. The unpleasant surprises of life should not be a reason to give up and forget about the plan.

Furthermore, all self-improvement plans are more likely to succeed if there is enough support system from the people around. Family, friends and other loved ones play an important role as they can easily push one forward should discouragement arise. Although any self-improvement effort begins with the self, one should still realize the fact that everyone is interdependent.

As self-improvement is not an easy task, it will further boost one's morale to continue in spite of difficulties if every simple success is celebrated. Each milestone, no matter how minor it is, is still one step towards the success of the entire self-improvement plan. Such celebration emphasizes further that it is totally possible to improve and be a better person.

There is indeed something more to life that every person is entitled to discover and unleash. It is really not a matter of luck. People are not successful or happy just because they are lucky. Instead, those who have improved selves are those who are willing to exert extra effort and are not afraid to constantly stand up in times of difficulties. They believe in themselves and their capacity to bring out their full potential.

Leadership Exposed

The literature written on leadership is phenomenal. The guide lines, tips, styles and profiles of exceptional leaders during the course of history, just to name a few areas of leadership. As we read and research, we learn to recognize specific leadership ideas and qualities we previously failed to see before. Following is a list of things we thought we knew and understood about leadership.

1) Leaders come in different styles.

History points us toward Albert Einstein, well known for his Theoretical Physics; Leonardo da Vinci, Known for his Art. These are leaders we use as mentors for their wisdom and experience or by their virtue and expertise, as well as what they contributed to society. Elders of a tribe or grandparents could be included in this category of informal leadership. Then you come up against the 'formal' leaders or those appointed or elected to the position of leadership.
Senators, congressmen, presidents or judges fall into this category; those who are elected to the position of eldership within a government or club.

Literature written by Lewis outlines the three basic styles of leadership which are authoritative, participative and delegative.

Then there is literature written by Likerts which outlines the four styles: authority that is exploited, authority that is charitable, deliberative and participative.

Also, included in the list of literature written by Goleman, who researches six styles of leadership; visionary, instructive, networking, democratic, commanding and pace making.

2) Leadership is a process of 'coming into'.

Some people seem to be born with leadership qualities, while others learn the art of leadership. However you come into these qualities, you need to develop and sharpen these leadership abilities. You can obtain knowledge by attending seminars, workshops and conferences on leadership. Another way to increase your abilities is to interact with people who already project and practice these leadership qualities.

Expanding your knowledge and exposure will enable you to obtain and exercise leadership attitudes, insights, and intergrading the cycle of learning. Being a leader is a full time, lifelong learning process; not something you accomplish over night. A good leader puts his or her knowledge , skills and attitudes to the test daily; plus, sets a goal to have a new experience each day.

3) Leadership begins with You.

First, applying the knowledge you accumulated to your own life is the best way to develop leadership abilities. Leaders enjoy the limelight. Remember your actions affect your credibility; as in 'action speaks louder then words'. How you interact with family, friends, co-workers or the public; connect with your actions and development as a leader. Time management in both your personal and professional responsibilities will affect your leadership qualities, too.

Repetition develops habits; habits form character. '7 Habits of Highly Effective People' by Steven Covey, a must read for insight on achieving personal leadership.

4) Leadership is shared.

Leadership is designed to be a shared responsibility between members of a group or team. Each individual must fulfill his or her responsibilities. Elected or 'formal' leadership positions are merely additional responsibilities from their usual team or group responsibilities. Being and effective leader means sharing the work. Putting a group of individuals together, forming members and leaders to work toward one mutual goal; is the formation of a great team. While learning to work together; there must be trust within the full group to be effective. Through actions the foundation of mutual respect and trust are built, which in turn builds confidence.

5) Leadership styles connected to situations.

Where dictatorship works in Singapore; it does not work in the United States of America. Leadership styles used in 'formal' leadership depends greatly on culture, beliefs, values and the form of government in that nation. There are no restrictions on the number of leadership styles used for any given situation. Most of the time, a combination of styles are used as the situation dictates.

In instances of war and calamity, decision-making is a matter of life and death; a nation's leader cannot afford to consult with all departments to arrive at crucial decisions. Leadership is different in times of peace and order, each sector and branch of government can freely work together and positively affect each other while working toward the mutual goal set before them.

Another situation would be leadership within an organization. When there is a high motivation and competent level; a combination of delegative and participative styles of leadership is in order. However, if the competence and commitment is low, a combination of high coaching, supporting and directing style of leadership is required.

The ideas we may already know or concepts we take for granted are actually the most useful insights we can have on leadership. How we apply these insights to our life is the difference between a good leader or a great leader.

When You Give You Succeed

The gift of giving is the true meaning of success. There are great lessons to be learned from one simple act.

One must understand and accept "the power of giving" is an extremely powerful act; which, in turn, will draw success and abundance in the life of the giver. When performed unselfishly and unconditionally, with no expectations, it will create a magnetic force within your whole being and effect you life; taking place in the center of your existence, mentally, physically and spiritually. In addition, you will feel a great sense of fulfillment.

The universal laws of spiritual, as well as, scientific are controlled by the acts of "giving and receiving".

In the spiritual realm "you will harvest what you sow" and "don't get tired of helping others, you will be rewarded when the time is right" this is from the book of Galatians. Scientifically, Isaac Newton's theory, affirms the spiritual realm, "for each action there is an equal reaction". Both spiritually and scientifically, these laws incorporated into one's daily life, you will attract and create the abundance and success in which you desire. The act of giving will lead to success.

Where most people view giving, connected to money; the true meaning of giving goes way beyond money. Allowing the fact, most donating is in the terms of money; one will usually find money scarce. The mere though or act of giving tests our misconceived beliefs and awareness about inadequacy. The amount we give, whether monetary or otherwise, does not measure our true worth.

Giving is a selfless, directly from the heart, act that can be very empowering as well as rewarding. Not connected to any holiday celebration, birthday or any special occasion but an act of compassion. Giving completely and unconditionally, to show gratitude and that you care and for no other reason; especially, not to expect something in return. Giving in this form, signals positive reactions; sets fire to your inner power and transmits positive energy that will draw a positive response from those around you. this message you unconsciously send out, will produce a chain reaction of positive events in your life, leading you to true success.

The chain reaction can be overwhelming at times, but it will be very rewarding as well. Those who share in this process will reap the rewards of their acts of giving, just as you have.

Simply and unconditionally giving, with complete acceptance and realizing you have plenty.

You can trust you will always have enough for all your needs. This compassionate act of giving develops a bond and very close union with your higher power, universe, spirit, God or your supreme authority. This connection is referred to as trusting in you higher power. You believe and trust in God, you will always have plenty; more than you need and the more you can give to help others. The greater your success will be.

The recipients of these selfless acts will in turn earn you, their love and respect. People, in general, have the need and desire to return acts of kindness that they have received. You will feel confident someone will be there for you, to help, because you first helped them.

Remember, your acts of kindness are unconditional; you should not expect anything in return from those you help. From the goodness of your heart, share and you will be rewarded. Make your reason for giving be the intense feelings of happiness and fulfillment. Your higher power will pour out blessings upon you at the right moments in your life, in a way only he can, beyond any earthly understanding. When you reach out and give a helping hand, share and act of kindness, donate in a time of need; you will feel an overpowering sense of joy. You will know the feeling of true success.

It is scientifically proven; you will enjoy a healthier, prolonged life when you receive that feeling of inner accomplishment and peace. Life becomes more enjoyable when you incorporate a healthy habit of giving.

Always engage in giving from the heart; don't allow fear and selfishness be your guide. Be thankful and be aware of all the miracles that occur instantly in your life. With the true gift of giving you will succeed.

Human nature and giving have a solid bond. When you engage in this simple act, you discover joy and fulfillment; as well as, attract an abundance of blessings. These blessings will in turn, lead to true success in all forms.

Get Organized: Your Finances

Many of us would love to save money. However, if you were to ask most people why they have so little at the end of the month there likely answer would be , I don't know. Many of us pay bills automatically and have no idea where, when or how much is coming out. The first step in solving this problem is to get you finances organized. It is quite easy to do and you don't have to spend hardly anything.

Many of us see advertised on television, expensive computer programs guaranteed to get your finances in order. Although these likely do what they are intended, they are costly. Why spend hundreds of dollars when you can do the same thing for almost nothing. All you need is a pen and paper. By simply looking at your ban statement, writing down your bills, how much goes out and when, you'll be taking the first step in getting your finances organized. IF you want to go high tech, you can create a spread sheet on your home computer. Leave the software and do it your self.

Something else that people are prone to buy are organizers. These range between 10-20 dollars. It is true that some kind of filing system is needed to keep track of bills as they come and when they get paid. However, you can make your own for next to nothing. Check to see if you have any plastic wallets lying around. If not you can purchase a package of about 100 for about 1.50$. Check to see if you have an old ring binder or folder. Again, if not these are available in most book stores for 2-3$. Simply store the bills in here and mark as they get paid. This filing system works just as well as those expensive organizers that you can purchase.

Organized finances are the first step in getting your financial status into shape. One you have a list of all out goings, and when they come off of your account, you'll either see improvement or where any financial problems lie. Make sure everything is included and the dates are correct and in chronological order. Before you know it you'll be on your way to a better financial future.

How To Shop, organize yourself and your children

Despite the many advancements of today's world, many of us still do not know how to shop properly. We always leave the store with to much or too little. Buying too much means that some could possibly spoil, wasting money. Buying to little means another trip to the store, wasting fuel. The answer to this problem seems simple, make a list. However, you need to put time into shopping lists or the wrong things get purchased.

Before you get that pencil and paper put, put your self into the correct room, the kitchen. As your making your list, you can actually check through and see what you are getting low on. You can see if certain items need to be replenished or if they can wait another week. A good, accurate list will keep unnecessary items from being bought and needed items from being forgotten.

Paperwork, for some reason seems hard to part with. Not many of us get emotionally attached to documents, but we fear the day we may need that particular document for reference. The first thing you should do is get everything into stacks. Take everything out such as passports, birth certificates, marriage certificates and tax returns.

Put your stacks into boxes and put the date of 1 year from today on the top. If the year passes and you not had to look in the box, chuck it. You won't likely need it.

Finally, our lovely children can be organizational nightmares. Getting them off to school alone can be a mammoth task. Something that may help is a large plastic or wicker laundry basket. Before your children go to bed make them fill that basket with everything they need for the next day. All of their gym clothes, books ect. Whatever they are going to need to get them through the day. This will make the items easy to access making the whole morning go faster. It will also teach your child responsibility and organizational skills.

By implementing these tips, you life and the life of your children can be organized and much less stressful.

Directions, Warranties, Receipts

How many times has something broken in your home? If your normal, likely loads. Many times items can be repaired but you have no idea where you left the assembly instructions. Without these, even with the replacement part, the item is now useless. This means it needs to be thrown out and replaced with something new. This wastes money and resources.

This happens also with items that cannot be repaired. How many times have you bought something and got it home to find it was broken. Either that or it breaks within its warranty period. The problem comes when you have no idea where the receipt or warranty evidence is. Again, this results in good money being wasted.

A good thing you may want to try is designating a drawer or cupboard to these types of items. Warranties and directions will fit nicely into kitchen drawers making them easy to locate. Receipts should be first placed in a large sized envelope and then placed in the drawer. Everything should be clearly labeled including the drawer itself. If at all possible. Do not put anything else in that drawer or things will start to get lost.

Having the ability to find these things quickly will save a lot of time and heartache. The kitchen makes the perfect place because it is one of the most frequently used rooms in the house. Nearly everyone in the family will go in there at one point of another during the day, and having that drawer clearly labeled will constantly remind family members where those documents, you never thought you would need are located.

Keeping documents safe and in a visible place is a great idea for keeping the home organized. Using a kitchen drawer will keep things out of the way but serve as a constant reminder where those needed documents are.

Remembering All Those Little Things

How many times have you gotten home from work and realized you had forgotten to do some important chore? By the time you realized it, it is too late is has to be put off until another day. How many times have you forgotten to do something because, it was scheduled months prior but when the date roles around, you have completely forgotten about it. This happens to all of us at some point in our lives. We get caught up in the daily grind of life and our routines so anything that happen outside of that runs a great risk of getting missed. In this article we will look at some ways to remind yourself of those little day to day chores and errands and to help remind your self of those events coming up in the next few months.

Many of us need just reminding to do those chores and errands after work. There are various things you can try. You don't need to invest loads of money in expensive software or hire a PA. You can do it with things you likely have in your home. The most basic tool is the little notebook and pen. Make sure you have this with you at all times and jot down those things you need to do that day. Always have it in your pocket as a reminder. Try to stay away from little scraps of paper. These frequently get lost making them useless.

If you have email or voice mail on your computer, try sending yourself messages. This is easy to do and takes just seconds. You can also set it up to send you messages while you are at work. Finally, if you have an answering machine in your home, phone it and leave yourself a reminder message. This is one of the first things we do when we arrive in our homes is check our messages. Should you forget during the day but are reminded as soon as you walk in. you may still have time to complete the chore that day.

Finally, what can you do about those dates that are due to come up in the future? Again, leave the high tech stuff alone. All you need is a small box and some index cards. Section the cards off according to month and label cards clearly with dates that something needs to be completed by. This is an excellent system for remembering those doctors and dentist appointments that are months away or some bill or other financial obligation.

By using these simple tips. The chances of you forgetting any important matters will greatly decrease.

How To Tackle The Big Tasks

How many times have we put off doing those large tasks because we know how much effort and energy they will require? Just thinking about doing them wears you down. Soon you find that this large job that you once had weeks to accomplish much be done in days. In this article we will look at ways to take on big tasks so they are more manageable. We will look and the best times of the day to tackle certain things to get them finished and checked off of your list.

Most big tasks can be broken up into small manageable tasks. To get then done with as little stress as possible, this is what should be done. If you're looking to spring clean your home, for example, divide the house up room by room. Then list everything that needs to be done in each room. Once you have your lists you need to prioritize what needs to be done first, second and so on. Once this is complete you can get going. Making lists of smaller tasks and ticking them off as you get them done gives you a feeling of accomplishment. Instead of one monster task you can reward yourself for doing the series of smaller tasks. You'll see things start to take shape and feel better as the task suddenly becomes smaller.

Big tasks in some ways are a mixed blessing. There are things that you like to do and things that you dread. When you have your list of what you want to get done for that day, if at all possible do the least desired task first. You energy levels are highest in the early part of the day so giving it to those tasks you really don't want to do will get them ticked off of your list much faster. Waiting until later, when you are tired and slow, will virtually guarantee that the task will get put off.

Big tasks seem quite daunting however; nearly all of them can be shattered into small tasks. By doing this you're making the large task much more manageable and even enjoyable at times. The next large task you know you have coming, pan in advance and break it up. You'll find it isn't so bad.

Finding Those Keys

Small objects are easy to misplace and lose.

This is likely most true of our keys. How often have you been ready to head out the door and are stopped in your tracks because you cannot find your keys. You turn the place up and down for hours until you locate them in the last place you had left them. We can all relate to this because it has likely happened at some point in our lives. This problem is quite easy to overcome with a little practice and formation of new habits.

If you're in a position that requires you to have a beeper then you're in a really good position to never lose your keys again. If you simply attach your beeper to your keeps, they next time you misplace them, activate your beeper. When the sound goes off you should be able to find your keys quite quickly. This can work for other small objects as well.

If you don't own a beeper then there are other things that you can try. Simply try putting a box for keys up so it is visible. Place near to the front or main entrance to your house, so it is the first thing you see as you come in and leave. Get into the habit of putting your keys in the box. Once you do it a few times it should start to become habit forming.

If you find your continually forgetting to put your keys in the box. Then some extra reinforcement might be needed. Get a roll of quarters, at least 20. Every time you put your keys in the box place a quarter in as well. Once you have done something 20 times it usually becomes a habit. However, if it still isn't sticking in your memory empty the quarters and start again. The quarters will serve as an extra reminder of where to put your keys until the habit is formed.

No one needs expensive equipment or software to organize and remember. All you need are simple devices and time to try to form new habits. Practice makes perfect and before you know it, you'll never be searching for those keys again.

Dealing With Paper And Interruptions

Daily, almost hourly it seems we get battered with messaged and demands on bits of paper. If that isn't bad enough, the phone is constantly going off forcing you to stop and re-start tasks. How are you expected to get things done with all of these forces working against you? In this article we will look at ways to keep the interruptions to a minimum while you try to sort your life out.

Most of us get something in the mail nearly everyday. If it isn't junk, it is bills or other things that need our attention. The highly organized person will check through their mail everyday and tackle those things immediately. Most of us just stuff it all in the drawer and wish it would go away. Something you can try is to get a small wicker or plastic basket. Make a deal with yourself. Put all of your mail in this small container and leave it. However, there are 2 conditions. The mail must still be visible and once the container is full you need to go through everything and tackle what needs to be done. This is effective for a few reasons. It does force you to look at your mail on a fairly regular basis. It also keeps it in a safe location so it is not cluttering up your house or office. Finally, keeping it visible will remind you it is there so it doesn't fall into the out of sight out of mind trap.

How many times have you set aside time to do things only to be interrupted by a constant barrage of phone calls. The more times you have to stop and re-start a task the less likely it will get done. The best thing to do is set aside some time to return phone calls. If the phone keeps ringing, let it ring. Let your answering machine do its job. If you like you can even put a message for callers stating you are otherwise engaged and will return calls at this time.

It is important not to let outside forces stop you from getting your tasks done. The more times you have to restart the less likely you will finish. By keeping the mail in a safe place and setting aside time to return phone calls, you can devote your time where you need to, getting your life sorted out.

Your Computer Needs Attention Too

With all of the pressure from environmental organizations on reducing waste, many have opted to go paperless and store documents on their computers. By doing this there is less clutter floating around your home and office. However, computers need to be organized as well. Simply saving things in the hard drive will quickly use up space and slow down you computers functions. Also, if you need to find something specific, you'll find it may take you hours, by the time you check through all of the existing saved documents.

If you have Microsoft word you have the ability to create files. If you have one computer in your home then have a file for each member of the family. These files will eventually get full so at various intervals through the year have a computer clear out. Tell everyone they have one week to sort their files or everything will get dumped. This way, all of the things that you need will be saved and the less important items can be discarded.

If you live on your own or want to clean up your work computer, folders can help with this as well. Just create folders for certain sections of your life. Perhaps bills, appointments and so forth. This way you can access tings easily without having to wade through years and years of old documents. Learn to use your folders section. You will be amazed how quickly things accumulate.

If you have a lot of things stored and genuinely need all of them, than consider getting some back up computer disks. Even though you may need everything, some things will still be more important than others. Keep the more important items saved on your computer and the others on disks. This way you can keep computer space free and still keep everything. Make sure you label your disks and keep a good filing system. This way you can still access what you need quickly.

With the pressure to go paperless, many of us forget to keep our computers organized. You need to keep on top of these things so you computer runs well and you can get to what you need.

Your Children's Room And Schoolwork

Children can be some of the worst organizers in the world. They have so much to keep track of between home and school that it is amazing anything get to you at all. Children's home and school work is important and keeping it organized is important. If things are neatly organized and easy to find you may find that your children start to enjoy doing their work and get it done quicker.

The first tip is for homework. Try setting aside a specific time for homework to be done. Make an agreement with your child that between these hours, it is homework and nothing else. Make it a time when you are available so you can assist if necessary. If this habit is established early in their school years, when they get into high school, it will be much less of a chore to get them to do it. The next tip is to have an area designated for homework. Make sure it is quiet so your child can concentrate. Have a box with everything that they could possible need. Make sure there is paper, pencils or pens, markers, scissors, calculators, rulers and so forth. This will minimalist the, I don't have a pencil problems that waste time. Having this established will set a good tone about homework and get your child into good habits early.

Children have loads of school work. Teach them how to use a ring binder early in life. Devote a section to each subject and get dividers in separate colors. This sends a message to the brain and helps it create its own internal filing system. You may also get your child to make an illustration about their particular subjects, to be placed in the ring binder. Designate some time each week, ideally during homework time to go through the folder and discard what is no longer needed. This is a great way to teach your child organization and spend quality time with them.

Children accumulate loads of paper during their school years. Keeping it organized isn't such a chore. By designating time each day for homework, having equipment on hand and going through their binders on a weekly basis, your child will be organized and start to do better in school.

Keeping Papers And Other Items In Control

In the average household, there is more paper generated than a small business. Between bills, taxes receipts, warranties, your children's school work, one can see how quickly your can get snowed under. In this day and age we don't have to keep everything. There comes a time when you have to discard some things. However, for those things that you need to keep, they need to be organized and easy to get to.

Get some three ring binders from your local book store and start organizing those things you need. Section off the binder according to your needs. One section can be devoted to bills, receipts, directions and one section for each child. When you have something that you need to keep, such as tax returns, in it goes. When your child brings home a great piece of school work then place it in their section. Keeping these items separate and in one place will make them easy to access and find. If your child doesn't know what to keep and what to throw away, tell them to keep one piece from each month of the year. This way you and your child can gage their progress.

Kitchens for some reason seem to attract miscellaneous items. Anything from loose nails, to recipes, to tacks. Something you can do to keep this under control and recycle is to use clear glass jars for storage. Once you are finished using them, give them a good clean and use them for pencils, paper clips or anything you find a lot of with no designated place. The clear jars are great because you can see into them, negating the need for labels. You can also try getting some Velcro strips to attach to the bottoms. This way they will stay in their shelf or other place reducing the risk of breakage.

No one needs expensive equipment to get organized. 9 times out of 10, what you will need is already in your home. By using simple and easy methods, you can organize your paperwork and store to miscellaneous items safely.

It Isn't Rocket Science

Getting things organized is quite important. Nearly every aspect of our lives functions better when we have things in their proper place. Getting organized is also quite easy, however many people let many parts of their lives fall into complete chaos. In this article we will talk about tome says to get your life in order, without having to spend loads of money or expend tons of effort. With some simple helpful hints that you can practice, you will soon see your life getting organized.

Organization of finances

One of the most important areas in our lives is our finances. It is vitally important that we keep track of how much money is coming in and going out of our accounts. The vast majority of those with money problems have seriously disorganized finances as well. Organization won't make the bills go away, but devising a plan of action is much easier when everything is in place.

Many spend hundred of dollars on expensive computer programs to organize their accounts. The truth is you don't need any of this. All you really need is a list of bills, their amounts and the dates they are due. You need to mark them off as they are paid and adjust your account accordingly. If you want to keep you bills in an organized way, get a binder and some plastic wallets or folders. Divide each section according to the type of bills and store them in there. This way they won't cause clutter and they will be easily accessible if you ever need them.

You may also be able to store this information on your computer. By simply creating folders, you can store your financial information in a paperless machine.

By using some simple and inexpensive techniques, you can quite quickly get your finances into order. This will result in more money in your account and fewer financial hassles.

Warranties, Receipts, Instructions

Most of the things that we buy have a clock attached to them. In other words, they will eventually break or stop working someday. When this happens, will you know where the warranty or receipt is? You may be entitled to a refund or compensation for repairs. However, you cannot prove this without your documents.

Have you ever assembles something only to have it break a few weeks or months later. You search for those instructions to see where you went wrong but they are no where to be found. This happens quite often, leaving the item useless.

There is a simple solution to this dilemma. If you have space in your kitchen, designate one of the drawers for your warranties, receipts and instructions. Label it clearly so you're constantly reminded of where those tings are. Warranties and instructions usually fit nicely into this space, receipts however may need to be placed in an envelope first.

The kitchen is a great place because everyone goes in there each day for one reason or another. Everyone will be reminded on a daily basis where those things you never though you would need are stored.

By designating a space for these items, you will know where they are and be able to get to them quickly and easily when the time comes.

Errands

We all need reminding at some time or another. How many times have you left work, arrived home and remembered all of the after work errands you were supposed to have done? By the time you have remembered, it is too late and these chores will have to be done another day. This has happened to everyone; we get caught up in the daily grind of work and home and forget anything else. Fortunately, reminding yourself of these things can be quite easy.

The simple and cheapest thing that you can do is carry a small notebook and pen with you. Make sure it is on you at all times. Write down the things that you need to get done and keep it in your pocket. It will act as your reminder. Avoid doing the same thing on bits of paper. These are to easy to loose making the errand easy to forget.

If you have email or voice mail, try sending yourself messages. You can arrange to have the messages sent to you thought the day at work, so you're constantly reminded. This will keep what you have to do fresh in your mind so you're not likely to forget.

Finally, if you have an answering machine at home, call and leave your self reminder messages. One of the first things we do when we arrive home is check for phone messages. If we are reminded in time, we may still have time to do it that day.

No one needs to spend a fortune on calendars or hire personal assistants to organize our lives. Chances are you have all of the technology you need right in your own home. By taking time to remind yourself, your errands will get done and you'll have more time to yourself.

Handling Big Tasks

Big tasks can be very daunting. Sometimes the mere though of them can make you feel tired. However, they must be done and done well. They next time your faced with a huge task, try planning it in advance. The reason being, you can organize your big task into several small tasks.

If you're for example having to clean your entire house for guests or other reasons, start planning ahead. Divide the house room by room and make a list of everything that needs to be done. Tick off every individual item as it gets done. This will give you a feeling of accomplishment. As you move through the house, your start to see things take shape which will inspire you to get more done.

Big tasks are usually a mixed blessing. They will be made up of things you enjoy doing as well as things that you dread. If your can, attack those things you dread first. Do them early in the day when your energy level is high. This will get them done quicker and allow you to do the more enjoyable things later.

Leaving the less desirable items until late in the day will virtually guarantee they won't get accomplished. This will lead to them being put off until a later date, if they get done at all.

Nearly every big task can be shattered into loads of small tasks. They key is starting ahead of time and planning. By doing this your big tasks will not seem so daunting.

Handling Papers And Interruptions

Even though were under constant pressure to go paperless, it still seems to consume a large part of our space. Many of us shove it into a drawer and hope it disappears while others of us just make lovely stacks. In an ideal world, we would open all of our mail and deal with the issues immediately. However, we don't live in an ideal world. However, there is a good middle ground that most of us can achieve. Try purchasing a small wicker or plastic basket. When your mail comes, place it in there. You can do this on two conditions. You need to keep your mail visible. In other words don't cover it up and when it gets full you must go through and deal with it. This is effective because it keeps the paper in one place, and forces you to attend to business on a fairly frequent basis.

Paperwork can consume us if we are not careful. For some reason we cannot bring ourselves to throw a lot of it away. None of us are particularly attached to paperwork but we fear the day we might actually need that document and have thrown it out. Here is what you can do. Gather up your paperwork into nice stacks. Take out things such as tax returns, marriage, divorce and birth certificates, passports and tax returns. Once those items are separated, box up the rest. Put the date, one year to the current date at the top of the box. If the year passes and you haven't had to go into the box, chances are that you won't have to. It is safe to chuck it away.

Finally, how many times have you been getting on with tasks, only to be interrupted with a series of phone calls? The more times you have to start, stop and restart a task the less likely you are to finish it. Do yourself a favor; set aside a time to answer your phone calls. If the phone keeps ringing, then let it ring. Let your answering machine or other family members take messages. If it is that important, they will call back.

Organizing isn't that difficult. Many times you just have to allow yourself time to get things done. Keep your time sacred for doing tasks and answer the calls at another time.

Using Kolb's Model To Set Goals

In 1984 a man by the name of David Kolb created a model based on the different ways that people learn. These learning styles have come to be known as "Kolb's model" and are used today to determine the different ways in which certain personalities learn and absorb information. When you're setting goals for yourself it can sometimes help to understand a bit more about the ways in which you, as an individual, learn.

Kolb believed that we learn by using four different styles of learning:

- Learning by doing, or by experimenting with something.

- Learning by watching and being conscious of the observing of something.

- Learning by feeling, or by actively experiencing something, and

- Learning by thinking and conceptualizing something.
  These four styles of learning can be broken

down even further by defining the type of "learner" a person is:

• The activist. This type of learner uses intuition and perception instead of reasoning to learn new things.

• The reflector. The reflector learns by watching and looking at the world from an entirely different perspective than other learners. These learners are highly imaginative and use this imagination to observe their own experiences.

• The theorist. This type of learner analyzes things logically and methodically. They look for a precise explanation of things as they are presented to them.

• The pragmatist. The pragmatist is a learner that uses the information they absorb in a practical way to further their knowledge. These types of learners are quick to get things done and are willing to take risks that other learners aren't willing to take.

When you know what category of learning that you best fit into you'll be able to determine what works best for you to achieve your goals. You'll have a better understanding of how you absorb information and what you can do with this processed information as it applies to goals.

Keep in mind that Kolb's model is just a sequence of learning theories and that many people will fall into more than one category when it comes to the way that they learn new things. As you start to set more goals for yourself you need to have a plan of how you are going to achieve these goals. Having goals is necessary but having the tools and the knowledge to reach these goals is just as important. After all, if you don't know what works best for you when it comes how you learn and grow how will you know what perceptions to follow and make a reality?

Set Lifetime Goals

One of the first things that you should think about when you're setting personal goals is what specific things you want to accomplish in your lifetime. These lifetime goals will give you the perspective that you need to shape many of the decisions that you'll be making in your life.

There are some specific areas of your life in which you're going to want to set very determined goals. The following categories will help you to focus on certain aspects of your lifetime goals:

• **Mental attitude**: Your mental attitude should be positive so that there are no negative thoughts or mindsets holding you back. Take a look at your behavior in certain situations and ask yourself if this was something that prevented you from reaching a specific goal.
• **Your career**: Depending on what career you want, there will be specific goals that you need to follow to make sure that you have all your credentials at the end of your schooling. Ask yourself what level it is that you want to reach in your career.

• **Family**: Setting family goals can be a bit more difficult than other goals because your decision will usually affect someone else as well. You'll first need to decide if you want to be a parent and if you want the responsibilities that come with parenting.

- **Financial**: Determine how much you want to be making when you reach a certain age.

- **Physical**: Determine if there are any athletic goals that you want to reach. This can be as simple as staying in good health or as complicated as learning how to mountain climb. What will it take for you to reach this physical goal?

• **Pleasure**: Make a list of things that make you happy. Then make another list of steps that you can take to incorporate more of these pleasures into your life.

Once you have a list of the above categories clearly written down you'll need to assign them with a priority number. Start with the number one priority and then start to implement changes in your life so that you can achieve this goal. Work down the list but keep in mind that you can change the priority of a category at any time. Your lifetime goals are the milestones that you want to reach for your own personal achievement. When you're setting lifetime goals it's important that you make decisions for yourself that are going to fit into the person you want to be. Perhaps the most important step when it comes to goal setting is to be firm in the lifetime goals categories that you feel are most important to you.

Determine Your Core Beliefs Before Settings Goals

Before you can set any goals for yourself you need to have a base of core beliefs that you live by. And your core beliefs are based on the cause and effect of the things that happen to you in your life. The way you feel will always be determined by an action that created the feeling. When it comes to goal setting you need to have a positive outlook on what is happening around you so that you can make good decisions for yourself.

The basic underlying concept of core beliefs and goals is that if you're not feeling and seeing the effects that you want to see you need to take a look at the reasons why. Once you make changes to the conditions that are causing you to fail to reach your goals you'll start to see the results that you want to see. This means making changes to the conditions within yourself, and within your life, which are keeping you from moving forward.

You, as an individual, need to take responsibility for when you feel uninspired and negative. This also means that you have the power to change these conditions of cause and effect. You need to feel that you CAN reach your personal and professional goals. But what does the cause and effect of what happens in your life have to do with being successful and reaching your goals? The answer is simple: When you are aware of the cause and effect of your own personal beliefs and goals you are better able to manage how you lead your life. Understanding and believing that you can be successful on a personal level leads to the belief that you can reach all of the goals that you set for yourself.

One of the most important things that you can do to reach your personal and professional goals is to cultivate and nurture your own personal power. Personal power is one of the most incredible allies that you can have when it comes to achieving success. Personal power is all about believing in yourself, your accomplishments, and your ability to reach your goals. When people have this personal power they become confident and motivated to go after the things they want in life. Just think of the rewards that you will receive when you have a great sense of personal power: there are no limits when it comes to the goals that you can reach.

One of the key aspects of personal power is the inner confidence to know that you can do anything you want to do. You can achieve the goals that you deserve because you have all the skills and techniques that you need to be successful. When you have personal power you have the assertiveness to do what's best for you and your professional career. It's this combination of confidence and assertiveness that is going to push you towards your goals and a help you achieve these goals.

Thank You For The Order

Michelle Kolin

CPSIA information can be obtained
at www.ICGtesting.com
Printed in the USA
LVHW081131070421
682791LV00050B/952

9 781802 176032